West Virginia Ecoregions

- ☐ Western Allegheny Plateau
- ■ Central Appalachians
- ▨ Ridge and Valley

Morgantown

Charleston

1. Good Zoo at Oglebay Resort
2. Ohio River Islands National Wildlife Refuge
3. North Bend State Park
4. Coonskin Park
5. Beech Fork State Park
6. Hawk's Nest State Park
7. Twin Falls Resort State Park
8. Pipestem Resort State Park
9. Bluestone State Park
10. Babcock State Park
11. Watoga State Park
12. Monongahela National Forest
13. Stonewall Jackson Lake State Park
14. West Virginia State Wildlife Center
15. Audra State Park
16. Canaan Valley Resort State Park
17. Blackwater Falls State Park
18. Sleepy Creek Wildlife Management Area
19. West Virginia Zoo
20. The Core Arboretum
21. Cranberry Mountain Nature Center
22. Schrader Environmental Education Center

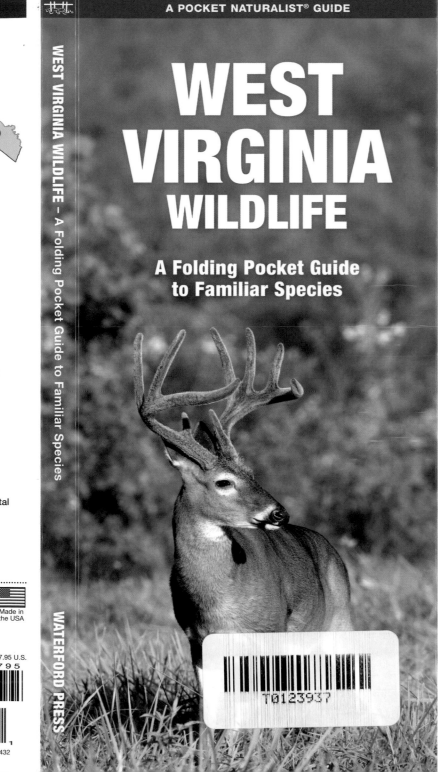

WEST VIRGINIA WILDLIFE

A Folding Pocket Guide to Familiar Species

WEST VIRGINIA WILDLIFE – A Folding Pocket Guide to Familiar Species

WATERFORD PRESS

T0123937

BUTTERFLIES & MOTHS

Eastern Tiger Swallowtail
Papilio glaucus
To 6 in. (15 cm)

Zebra Swallowtail
Eurytides marcellus
To 3.5 in. (9 cm)

Monarch
Danaus plexippus
To 4 in. (10 cm)
West Virginia's state butterfly.

Spicebush Swallowtail
Papilio troilus
To 4.5 in. (11 cm)

Black Swallowtail
Papilio polyxenes
To 3.5 in. (9 cm)

Cabbage White
Pieris rapae
To 2 in. (5 cm)

Spring Azure
Celastrina argiolus
To 1.25 in. (3.2 cm)

Eastern Tailed Blue
Cupido comyntas
To 1 in. (3 cm)

American Copper
Lycaena phlaeas
To 1.25 in. (3.2 cm)

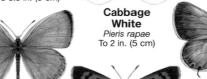

American Lady
Vanessa virginiensis
To 2 in. (5 cm)

Mourning Cloak
Nymphalis antiopa
To 3.5 in. (9 cm)

Large Wood Nymph
Cercyonis pegala
To 3 in. (8 cm)

Red Admiral
Vanessa atalanta
To 2.5 in. (6 cm)

Question Mark
Polygonia interrogationis
To 2.5 in. (6 cm)
Silvery mark on underwings resembles a question mark or semicolon.

Luna Moth
Actias luna
To 4.5 in. (11 cm)

INSECTS

Honey Bee
Apis mellifera
To .75 in. (2 cm)
West Virginia's state insect.

Field Cricket
Gryllus pennsylvanicus
To 1 in. (3 cm)

Green Stink Bug
Acrosternum hilare
To .75 in. (2 cm)

Ladybug Beetle
Family Coccinellidae
To .5 in. (1.3 cm)

Pyralis Firefly
Photinus pyralis
To .5 in. (1.3 cm)

Six-spotted Tiger Beetle
Cicindela sexguttata
To .5 in. (1.3 cm)

Green June Beetle
Cotinus nitida
To 1 in. (3 cm)

Paper Wasp
Polistes spp.
To 1 in. (3 cm)
Hanging paper-like nests are made by females from wood pulp and saliva.

Japanese Beetle
Popillia japonica
To .5 in. (1.3 cm)

Carolina Locust
Dissosteira carolina
To 2 in. (5 cm)

Katydid
Pterophylla camellifolia
To 2 in. (5 cm)
Loud 2-part call – *katy-DID* – is heard on summer evenings.

White-tailed Dragonfly
Plathemis lydia
To 2 in. (5 cm)

Yellow Jacket
Vespula spp.
To .5 in. (1.3 cm)
Black and yellow with banded abdomen. Can sting repeatdly.

Dragonfly
Suborder *Epiprocta*
To 3 in. (8 cm)
Most dragonflies rest with their wings held open.

Praying Mantis
Mantis religiosa
To 2.5 in. (6 cm)

Familiar Bluet
Enallagma civile
1.5 in. (4 cm)

Ebony Jewelwing
Calopteryx maculata
To 1.7 in. (4.5 cm)
Like most damselflies, it rests with its wings held together over its back.

FISHES

Brook Trout
Salvelinus fontinalis To 28 in. (70 cm)
West Virginia's state fish.

Rainbow Trout
Oncorhynchus mykiss To 44 in. (1.1 m)

Smallmouth Bass
Micropterus dolomieu To 27 in. (68 cm)
Jaw joint is beneath the eye.

Largemouth Bass
Micropterus salmoides To 40 in. (1 m)
Jaw joint extends beyond the eye.

Spotted Bass
Micropterus punctulatus To 2 ft. (60 cm)

Flathead Catfish
Pylodictis olivaris To 5 ft. (1.5 m)
The largest game fish in West Virginia, it can exceed 50 pounds.

Rock Bass
Ambloplites rupestris To 17 in. (43 cm)
Their bright red eyes have earned them the nickname, "redeyes."

White Crappie
Pomoxis annularis To 20 in. (50 cm)

Freshwater Drum
Aplodinotus grunniens To 3 ft. (90 cm)
Also called white perch.

Yellow Perch
Perca flavescens To 16 in. (40 cm)

Bluegill
Lepomis macrochirus
To 16 in. (40 cm)

Common Carp
Cyprinus carpio To 30 in. (75 cm)

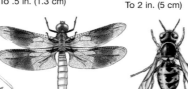

Muskellunge
Esox masquinongy
To 6 ft. (1.8 m)

Walleye
Sander vitreus To 40 in. (1 m)
Note white spot on lower lobe of tail.

REPTILES & AMPHIBIANS

Spring Peeper
Pseudacris crucifer
To 1.5 in. (4 cm)
Note dark X on back. Musical call is a series of short peeps.

Wood Frog
Lithobates sylvaticus
To 3 in. (8 cm)
Note dark mask. Staccato call is duck-like.

Pickerel Frog
Lithobates palustris
To 3 in. (8 cm)
Call is a snore-like croak lasting up to 3 seconds.

Green Frog
Lithobates clamitans
To 4 in. (10 cm)
Single-note call is a banjo-like twang.

American Toad
Anaxyrus americanus
To 4.5 in. (11 cm)
Call is a high musical trill lasting up to 30 seconds.

Gray Treefrog
Hyla versicolor
To 2.5 in. (6 cm)
Call is a loud resonating trill.

Eastern Painted Turtle
Chrysemys picta picta
To 10 in. (25 cm)

Snapping Turtle
Chelydra serpentina To 18 in. (45 cm)
Note large head, knobby shell and long tail.

Eastern Fence Lizard
Sceloporus undulatus To 8 in. (20 cm)

Eastern Box Turtle
Terrapene carolina carolina
To 9 in. (23 cm)

Eastern Garter Snake
Thamnophis sirtalis sirtalis
To 4 ft. (1.2 m)
Light back and side stripes are well defined. Color varies.

Northern Water Snake
Nerodia sipedon To 4.5 ft. (1.4 m)
Note dark blotches on back.

Timber Rattlesnake
Crotalus horridus To 6 ft. (1.8 m)
West Virginia's state reptile.

Copperhead
Agkistrodon contortrix To 52 in. (1.3 m)
Venomous snake has hourglass-shaped dark bands on back.

Black Rat Snake
Elaphe obsoleta obsoleta
To 8 ft. (2.4 m)

BIRDS

Mallard ♂ ♀
Anas platyrhynchos To 28 in. (70 cm)

Wood Duck
Aix sponsa To 20 in. (50 cm)

Hooded Merganser
Lophodytes cucullatus To 20 in. (50 cm)

Blue-winged Teal ♀
Spatula discors To 16 in. (40 cm)

Canada Goose
Branta canadensis To 45 in. (1.14 m)

Great Blue Heron
Ardea herodias To 4.5 ft. (1.4 m) Note yellow bill and black feet.

Great Egret
Ardea alba To 38 in. (95 cm)

Green Heron
Butorides virescens To 22 in. (55 cm)

Killdeer
Charadrius vociferus To 12 in. (30 cm) Note two breast bands.

Ring-billed Gull
Larus delawarensis To 20 in. (50 cm)

Mourning Dove
Zenaida macroura To 13 in. (33 cm)

Rock Pigeon
Columba livia To 13 in. (33 cm)

Wild Turkey
Meleagris gallopavo To 4 ft. (1.2 m)

Ruffed Grouse
Bonasa umbellus To 19 in. (48 cm)

Ruby-throated Hummingbird
Archilochus colubris To 3.5 in. (9 cm)

BIRDS

Northern Flicker
Colaptes auratus To 13 in. (33 cm) Wing and tail linings are yellow.

Red-bellied Woodpecker
Melanerpes carolinus To 11 in. (28 cm)

Downy Woodpecker
Dryobates pubescens To 6 in. (15 cm) The similar hairy woodpecker is larger and has a longer bill.

Pileated Woodpecker
Dryocopus pileatus To 17 in. (43 cm)

Red-shouldered Hawk
Buteo lineatus To 22 in. (55 cm)

Red-tailed Hawk
Buteo jamaicensis To 25 in. (63 cm)

Cooper's Hawk
Accipiter cooperii To 20 in. (50 cm) Note long, rounded white-tipped tail.

Great Horned Owl
Bubo virginianus To 25 in. (63 cm) Call is a resonant – hoo-HOO-hoooo.

Barred Owl
Strix varia To 2 ft. (60 cm) Call is a loud – who-cooks-for-you? who-cooks-for-you-all?

Osprey
Pandion haliaetus To 2 ft. (60 cm) Found near water.

Bald Eagle
Haliaeetus leucocephalus To 40 in. (1 m)

White-breasted Nuthatch
Sitta carolinensis To 6 in. (15 cm)

Belted Kingfisher
Megaceryle alcyon To 14 in. (35 cm)

American Kestrel
Falco sparverius To 12 in. (30 cm)

Turkey Vulture
Cathartes aura To 32 in. (80 cm) Note red head and two-toned underwings.

BIRDS

Carolina Wren
Thryothorus ludovicianus To 6 in. (15 cm)

Eastern Kingbird
Tyrannus tyrannus To 8 in. (20 cm)

Blue Jay
Cyanocitta cristata To 14 in. (35 cm)

Barn Swallow
Hirundo rustica To 8 in. (20 cm)

Eastern Meadowlark
Sturnella magna To 9 in. (23 cm)

Red-winged Blackbird
Agelaius phoeniceus To 9 in. (23 cm)

Common Raven
Corvus corax To 27 in. (68 cm) Call is a hoarse croak.

European Starling
Sturnus vulgaris To 8 in. (20 cm)

American Crow
Corvus brachyrhynchos To 22 in. (55 cm) Call is a distinct – caw.

Tree Swallow
Tachycineta bicolor To 6 in. (15 cm)

Carolina Chickadee
Poecile carolinensis To 4.5 in. (11 cm)

Tufted Titmouse
Baeolophus bicolor To 6 in. (15 cm)

American Robin
Turdus migratorius To 11 in. (28 cm)

Wood Thrush
Hylocichla mustelina To 8 in. (20 cm) Note rusty head and spotted breast.

Eastern Bluebird
Sialia sialis To 7 in. (18 cm)

BIRDS

Gray Catbird
Dumetella carolinensis To 9 in. (23 cm) Note black cap and reddish undertail feathers.

Northern Mockingbird
Mimus polyglottos To 11 in. (28 cm)

Song Sparrow
Melospiza melodia To 7 in. (18 cm) Note central breast spot.

House Sparrow
Passer domesticus To 6 in. (15 cm)

Baltimore Oriole
Icterus galbula To 8 in. (20 cm)

Brown Thrasher
Toxostoma rufum To 12 in. (30 cm)

Common Yellowthroat
Geothlypis trichas To 5 in. (13 cm)

Dark-eyed Junco
Junco hyemalis To 7 in. (18 cm)

American Redstart
Setophaga ruticilla To 5 in. (13 cm)

Indigo Bunting
Passerina cyanea To 6 in. (15 cm)

House Finch
Haemorhous mexicanus To 6 in. (15 cm)

Eastern Towhee
Pipilo erythrophthalmus To 9 in. (23 cm) Cheerful song is – Drink-your-teeeeeeea!

Scarlet Tanager
Piranga olivacea To 7 in. (18 cm)

American Goldfinch
Spinus tristis To 5 in. (13 cm)

Northern Cardinal
Cardinalis cardinalis To 9 in. (23 cm) **West Virginia's state bird.**

MAMMALS

Virginia Opossum
Didelphis virginiana To 40 in. (1 m) Note long fur and naked tail.

Snowshoe Hare
Lepus americanus To 20 in. (50 cm) Coat is white in winter.

Eastern Cottontail
Sylvilagus floridanus To 18 in. (45 cm)

Tricolored Bat
Perimyotis subflavus To 3.5 in. (9 cm)

Woodchuck
Marmota monax To 32 in. (80 cm)

Eastern Chipmunk
Tamias striatus To 12 in. (30 cm) Note white stripes on side and face.

Eastern Gray Squirrel
Sciurus carolinensis To 20 in. (50 cm)

Red Squirrel
Tamiasciurus hudsonicus To 14 in. (35 cm)

Fox Squirrel
Sciurus niger To 28 in. (70 cm)

White-footed Mouse
Peromyscus leucopus To 8 in. (20 cm)

House Mouse
Mus musculus To 8 in. (20 cm) Introduced pest has a naked tail.

Meadow Vole
Microtus pennsylvanicus To 7 in. (18 cm)

American Beaver
Castor canadensis To 4 ft. (1.2 m)

Common Muskrat
Ondatra zibethicus To 2 ft. (60 cm) Aquatic rodent has a naked, scaly tail.

MAMMALS

Common Raccoon
Procyon lotor To 40 in. (1 m)

Northern River Otter
Lontra canadensis To 52 in. (1.3 m)

Long-tailed Weasel
Mustela frenata To 21 in. (53 cm)

Striped Skunk
Mephitis mephitis To 32 in. (80 cm)

Coyote
Canis latrans To 52 in. (1.3 m)

Mink
Neovison vison To 28 in. (70 cm) Chin is white.

Common Gray Fox
Urocyon cinereoargenteus To 3.5 ft. (1.1 m) Note black-tipped tail.

Red Fox
Vulpes vulpes To 40 in. (1 m)

Wild Boar
Sus scrofa To 6 ft. (1.8 m) Introduced species.

Bobcat
Lynx rufus To 4 ft. (1.2 m)

White-tailed Deer
Odocoileus virginianus To 7 ft. (2.1 m) Fluffy tail is white below and held aloft when running.

Black Bear
Ursus americanus To 6 ft. (1.8 m) **West Virginia's state mammal.**